Gg

Garden

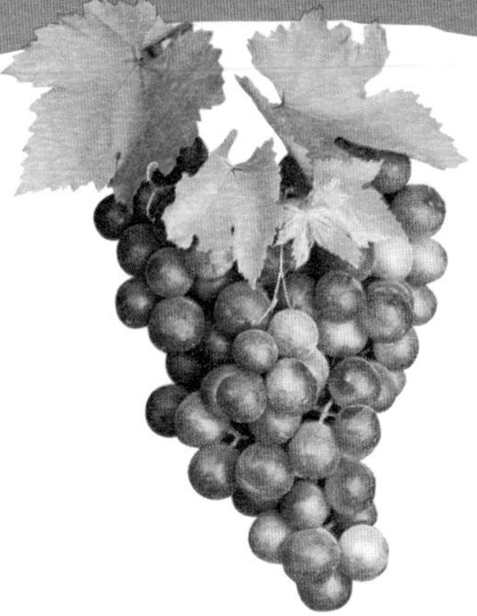

Written by Carolyn Necko

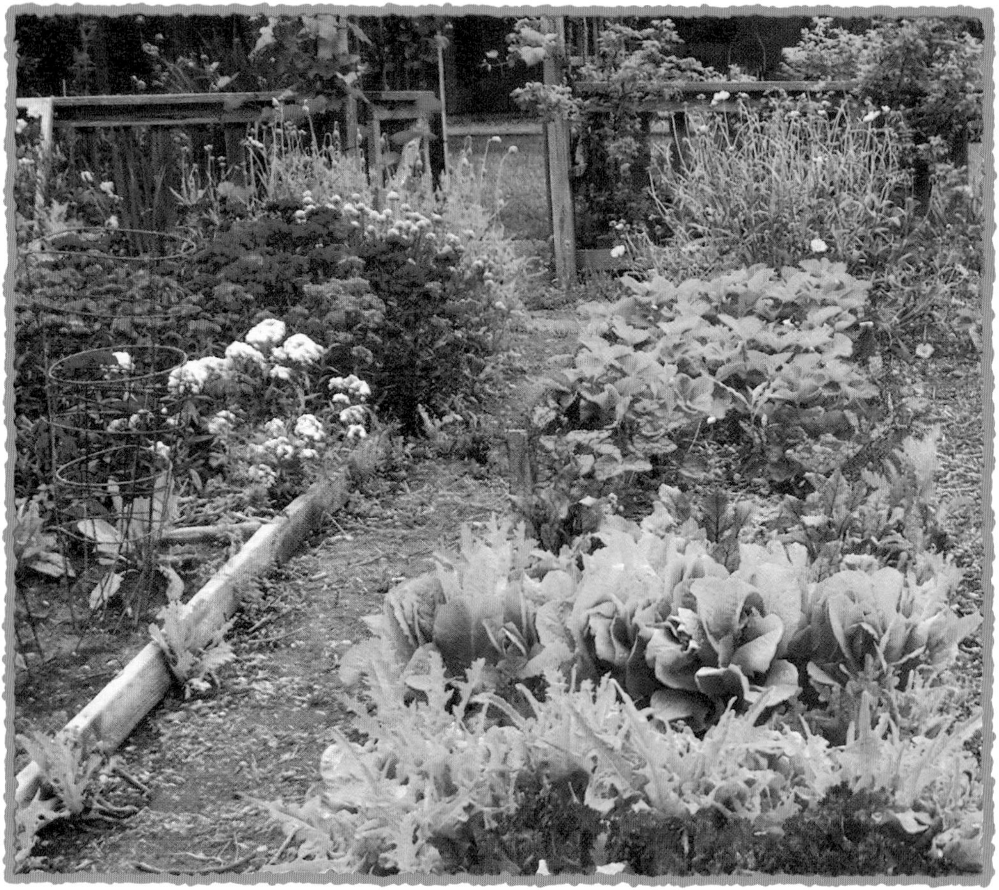

garden

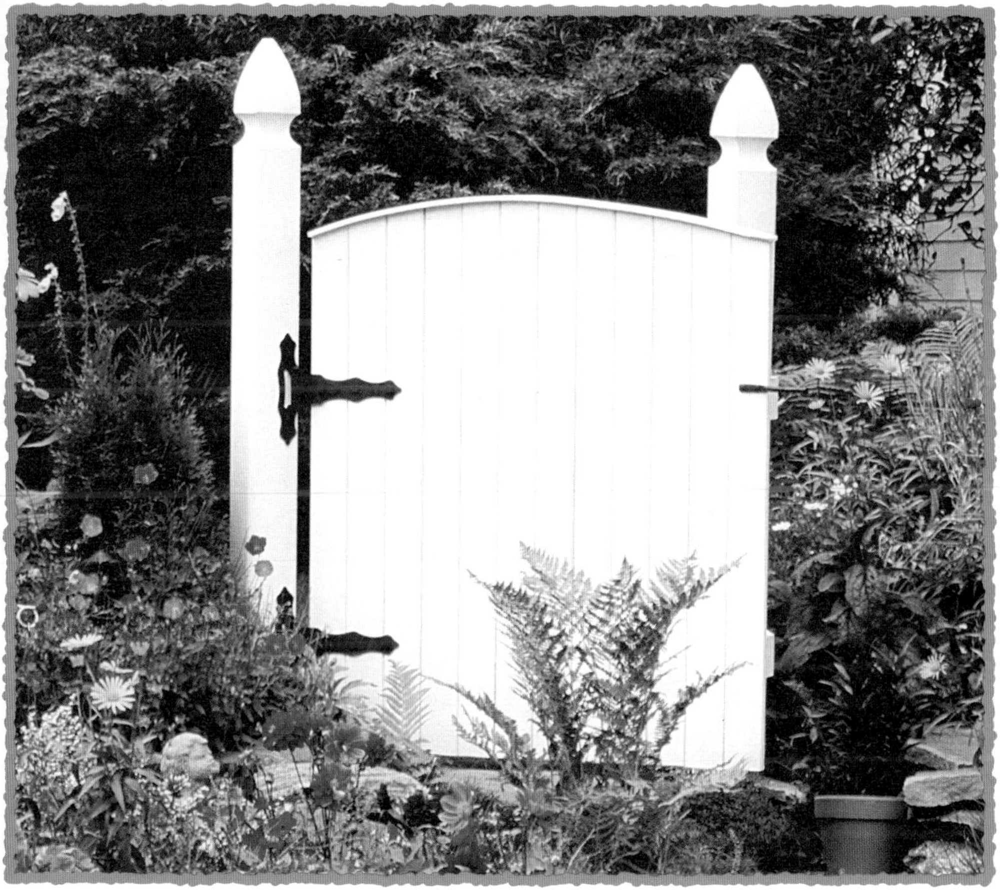

gate

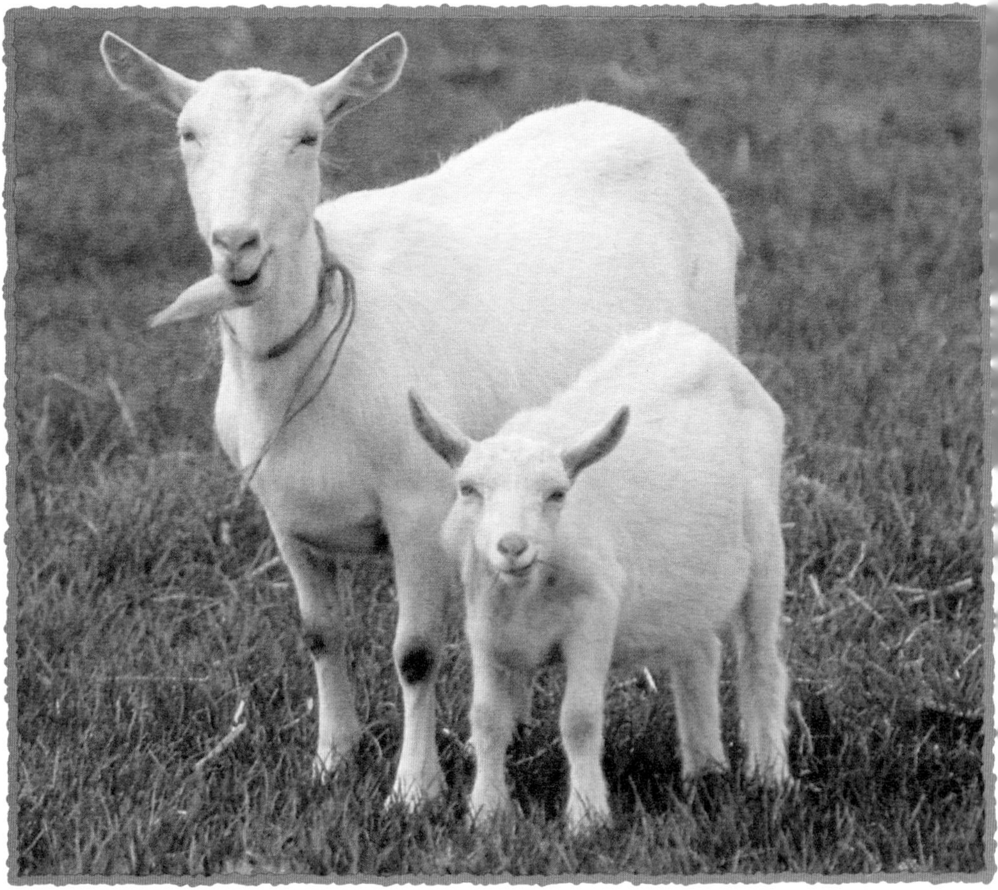

goats

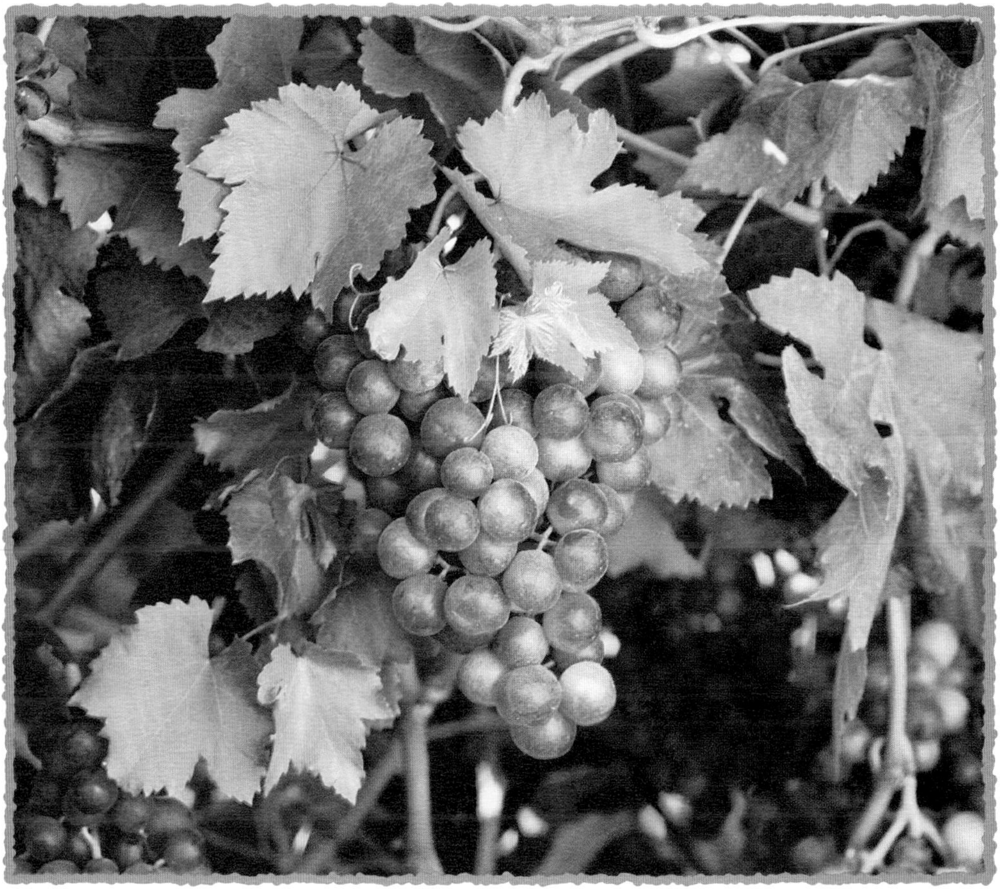

grapes

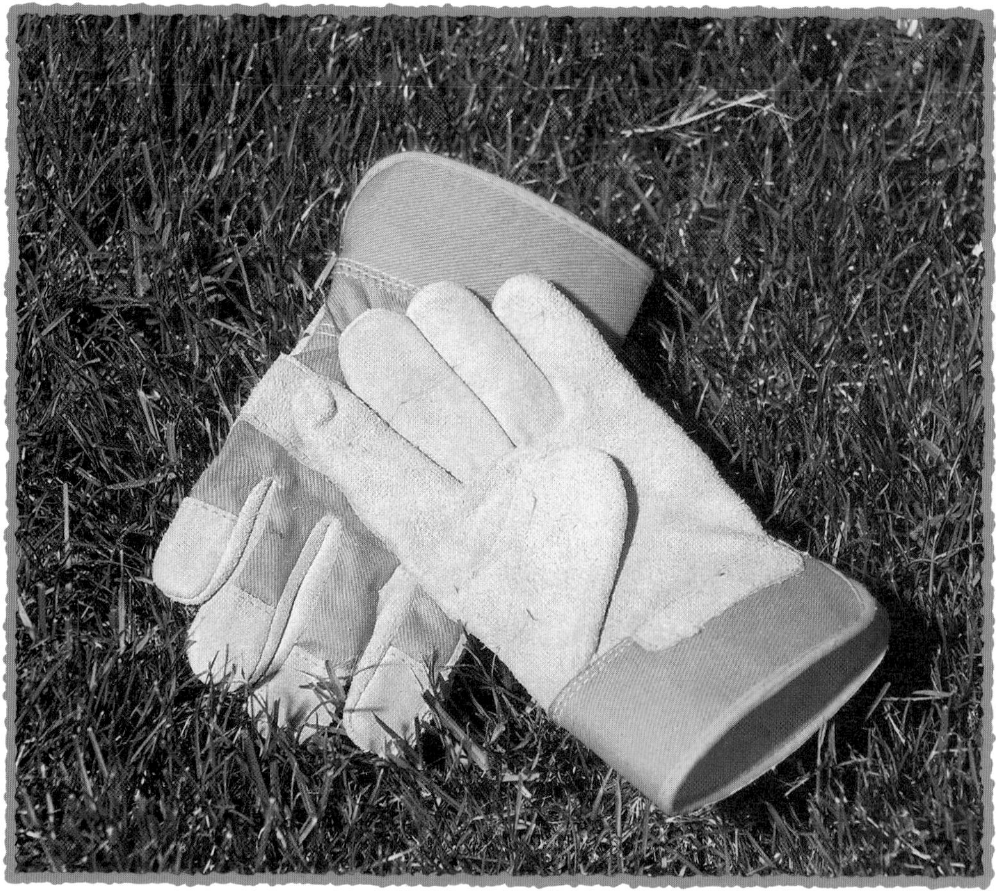

gloves

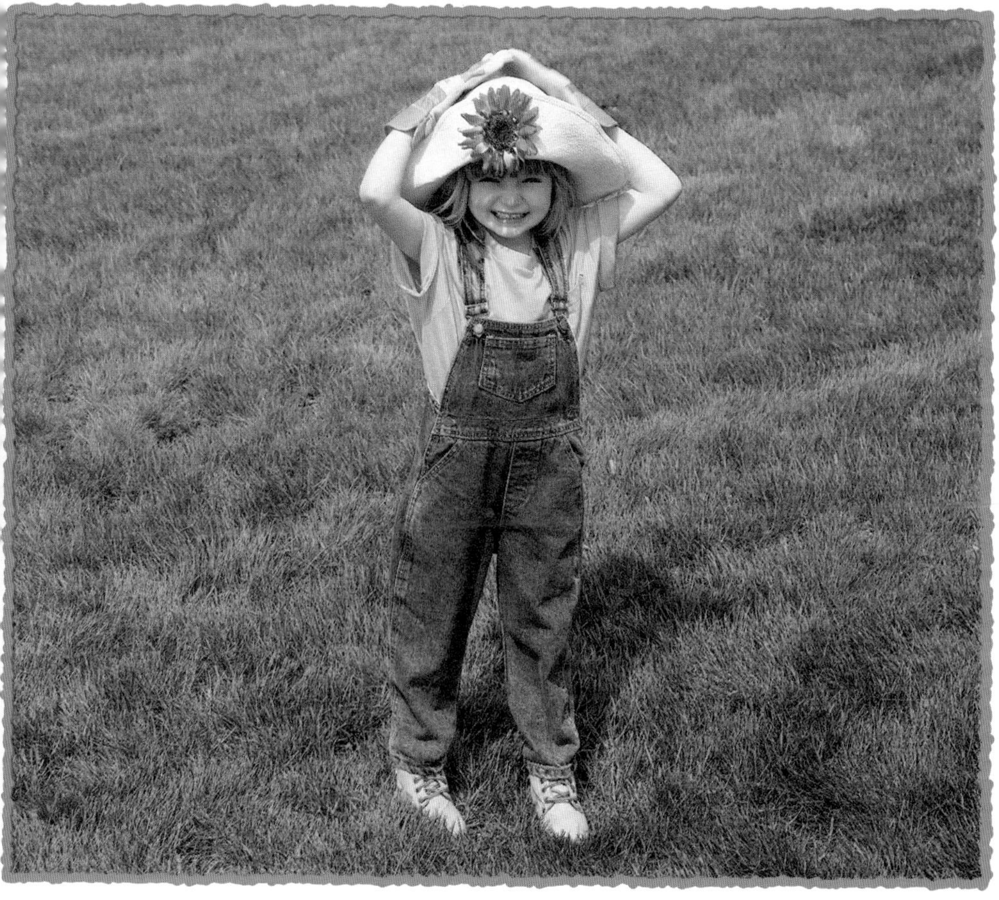

girl

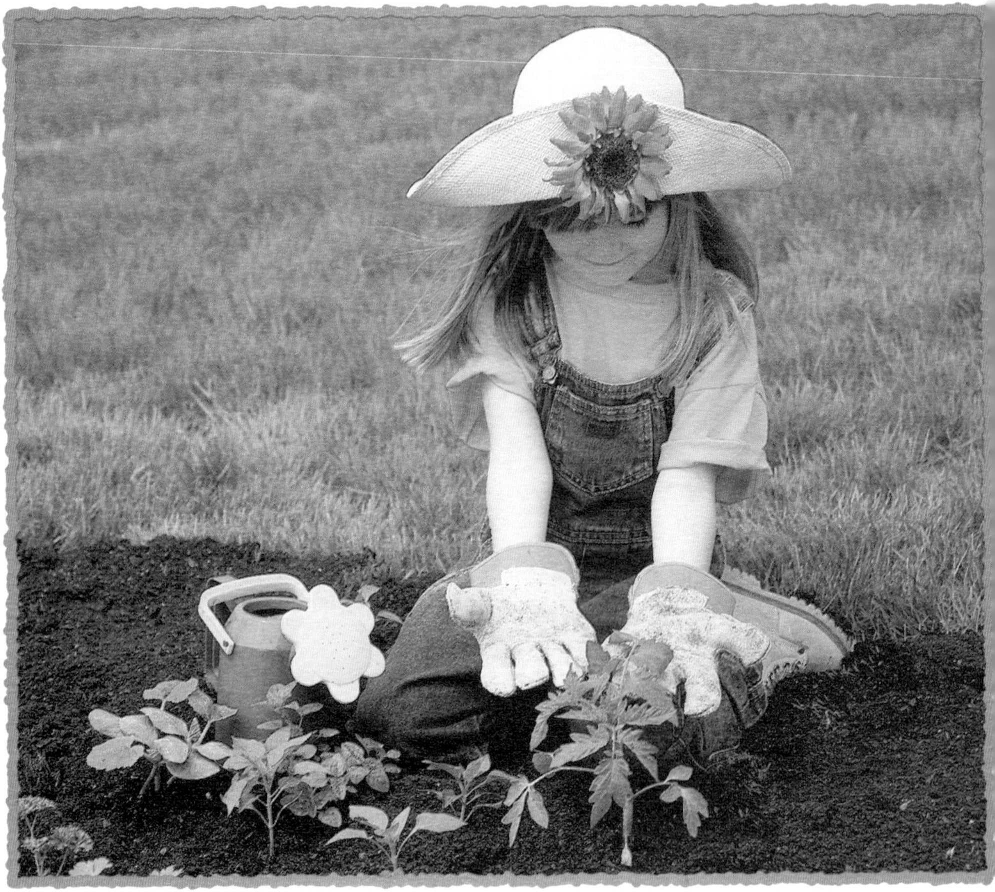

Grow!